Eastleigh

Steam Centre Of The South Western

By Barry J. Eagles

**For my friends
David and Doris Cox**

First Published 2002   ISBN 0 946184 93 3

ont cover: 'Schools' 4-4-0 No. 926 *Repton* stands in the erecting shop at
stleigh after cosmetic restoration. Photo 20th Oct 1966 by Barry J. Eagles

ck cover: Eastleigh MPD with No. 31831 heading a line-up on 5th May
63. Photo by Barry J. Eagles

ontispiece: Urie 'G16' 4-8-0 tank number 30495 displays its powerful front
d at Eastleigh. This massive tank engine was built at Eastleigh Works in
ugust 1921. Only four were built for shunting at the new marshalling yard
Feltham. Withdrawn in December 1962 after running 803,887 miles, it was
oken up at Eastleigh a month later. Photo taken on 18th December 1962 by
rry J Eagles.

Copyright Barry J. Eagles/Kingfisher Productions

Published By

Waterfront

A Division of Kingfisher Productions

The Dalesmade Centre, Watershed Mill, Settle,

North Yorkshire BD24 9LR

Printed by The Amadeus Press, Cleckheaton, West Yorkshire

Foreword

A fascinating spectacle was watching molten metal being poured in the foundry. The foundry men being protected by pieces of corrugated metal sheeting, no eye protection at all. The casting is quite large and could be a cylinder block. Photo taken on 4th August 1954 by Dick Sansbury

Sundays were a special day in the Eagles' household of the late 1950s and early 1960s, I would be up at 6:00 am for my Sunday morning paper round and be back home for bacon, eggs, sausages, and fried bread with Daddies sauce all washed down with copious cups of tea. At noon my hard working mother would have cooked the Sunday roast for my father, three sisters, brother and myself. Mum's roast beef and Yorkshire puddings were out of this world, no one thought of healthy eating in those days. At one o' clock after more cups of tea, I would stroll down to Millbrook station to catch a train to Eastleigh. Invariably it would be hauled by one of Maunsell's magnificent 'Lord Nelsons'. At Eastleigh station I would alight and walk up to Campbell Road railway bridge, pausing to look at the Hants and Dorset bus depot and a model shop window on the way. On top of the bridge I would peer into Eastleigh locomotive works yard which would contain ex-works locomotives and locomotives awaiting overhaul or repair. I would continue along Campbell Road passing the locomotive shed entrance until I came to number 34, the home of the genial Mr and Mrs Woods and their son David. Tommy Woods was a Yorkshire man who had served his apprenticeship at the London and North Eastern Railway works at Doncaster and had several fingers missing as a result of an accident there.

After yet more cups of tea he would tell me which locomotives were waiting to be scrapped or overhauled. He was foreman of the erecting shop at Eastleigh works and he would take me over to that great cathedral of steam: The British Railway's Southern Region Eastleigh Locomotive Works. I would be taken down the rows of steam engines in various states of repair, and would then visit the lines of engines waiting to be scrapped at the back of the works or the steam shed. If I saw a builders plate or number plate on an engine awaiting scrap, this would be officially removed ready for my collection at the next visit, the cost complete with official receipt for every item was £1.00, HAPPY DAYS! In the mid 60's, my great friend David Cox would pick me up in his Wolseley 680 and whisk me up to Eastleigh, luxury indeed!

Eastleigh works is now part of the Alstom Empire, after being owned by variants of British Railways' engineering services and even a worker's co-operative at one point. The separate carriage works is now a bus repair depot. The connection with those past days still remain as the Eastleigh Railway Preservation Society, of which I am a member, is currently overhauling the doyen of the 'Lord Nelson' Class No. 850

Lord Nelson himself, and my brother Martin Eagles is employed there. Open Days are a thing of the past, with the last such event being held in 1992 which co-incided with 'S15' No. 828's first year in steam after restoration.

The majority of the slides were taken by myself on a Pentax SV camera on 35mm Kodachrome II or X film. I must thank the Meon Valley Locomotive Society, of which I have the honour of being the only chairman since it was founded 32 years ago, for the use of the Dick Sansbury slides. Dick used to be a teacher at Eastleigh Grammar School, now Barton Peveril College. He was a friend of Stephen Collingwood Townroe, the Eastleigh Motive Power Superintendent, and they used to go on filming trips together. I must also mention another old friend George Wheeler. George filmed mainly in black and white with an Ensign folding camera, several of his photographs appeared in the various ABC's of the 1950's and 1960's. He took a few colour prints, the negatives of these being in my collection. Dick and George are no longer with us, but their work lives on.

Barry James Eagles   Chandler's Ford, April 2002

The Carriage Works was separate to the Locomotive Works and was on the East side of the main line and to the North of the Locomotive Works. A standard carriage is being worked on, behind is a carriage freshly painted in carmine and cream (blood and custard to the enthusiasts!). The carriage works closed in 1967, and is now a bus repair depot. Photo taken on 4th August 1954 by Dick Sansbury.

Introduction

Until September 1910, all the locomotives built for the London and South Western Railway were built at the company's Nine Elms works or by companies, such as Dubs or Neilson, both of Glasgow. In 1890 the London and South Western Railway Company moved its carriage works to Eastleigh from Nine Elms, which was in London. In 1909 the locomotive works followed and moved from Nine Elms to Eastleigh under the control of Dugald Drummond the London and South Western's Locomotive Superintendent, and his works manager Robert Urie, who both hailed from Scotland. When opened, the locomotive works employed 1,100 men, this along with the carriage work's 1,500 employees, made the London and South Western Railway the biggest employer of people in the area. The company built housing for their employees and today, nearly 100 years later, the housing in Campbell Road and other roads are still standing. From a small 'S14' class 0-4-0 tank No. 101 built in September 1910, 'till the rebuilding of 'West Country' class Pacific No. 34104 *Bere Alston* in May 1961, 321 steam locomotives were built, and 104 were rebuilt there.

Dugald Drummond died in 1912 and Robert Urie took over as Locomotive Superintendent. This likeable man held this post until the grouping of the railways in 1923. Robert Urie's locomotives were large, chunky, powerful machines with 4-6-0's of classes 'H15', 'N15' and 'S15', as well as the four 'G16' 4-8-0 tanks and the five 'H16' 4-6-2 tanks. Robert Urie's successor was Richard Maunsell from the Ashford works of the South Eastern and Chatham Railway. He improved Urie's 4-6-0s and had another 15 'H15' and 25 'S15's' built. At the suggestion of the Southern Railway's publicity manager Sir John Elliot, the 'N15's' became the famous 'King Arthur' Class. Maunsell stated that he had no objections but that it would make no difference to their performance. Eastleigh built another 24 and the North British Locomotive Company of Glasgow built another 30 of the 2 cylindered machines. Maunsell then designed the magnificent Lord Nelson 4 cylinder 4-6-0s and 'Schools' 3-cylinder 4-4-0s all of which were built at Eastleigh. Twenty 'U1' 3-cylinder 2-6-0s, five 'W' 3-cylinder 2-6-4 tanks and all 20 'Q' 0-6-0s completed the engines built by the time the well-liked Maunsell retired in 1937. During his regime seven 4-6-4 tanks from the London Brighton and South Coast Railway and seven 2-6-4 tanks to a South Eastern and Chatham design were rebuilt into tender locomotives.

Maunsell's successor was the brilliant Oliver Bulleid who designed the powerful 'Merchant Navy' class, all 30 of which were built and rebuilt at Eastleigh. Only six of the lighter but similar 'West Country's'/'Battle of Britains' were built at Eastleigh, the other 104 being built at Brighton works. All 60 rebuilt 'Light' Pacifics were completed at Eastleigh. By a strange coincidence the last steam locomotive built at Eastleigh 34104 *Bere Alston*, which was built there in April 1950, was the last locomotive rebuilt there in May 1961. Bulleid left the Southern in 1949. Just prior to that, in 1948, the railways were nationalised and the unconventional Bulleid Pacifics were rebuilt under the auspices of R.G. Jarvis into a more orthodox machine.

Eastleigh works is fortunate in having 23 of the engines built there and nine of the engines rebuilt there in preservation, several of which have returned to the main line over the past few years.

Bulleid 'Merchant Navy' Class No. 35006 *Peninsula and Oriental Steam Navigation Co.* stands outside Eastleigh shed in immaculate ex-works condition. She was built at Eastleigh in December 1941 and was rebuilt there in October 1959. On the 4th June 1942 she was named at Ashford works by Sir W. Currie, Chairman of P & O. Withdrawal came in August 1964 after running 1,134,319 miles. She spent 18 years in Woodhams' scrapyard at Barry before being purchased and moved to the Gloucester Warwickshire Railway at Toddington where she is being restored. Photo taken on 5th September 1953 by Dick Sansbury

The South of England rarely has heavy snowfalls, but they do occur from time to time as this picture taken from the Campbell Road bridge shows. Two 'Z' 0-8-0 tanks Nos. 30955 and 30956 with an unidentified narrow cab 'T9' 4-4-0, wait to venture out on to the mainline. Both 'Zs' were constructed at Brighton works in 1929. No. 30955 was broken up at Eastleigh in April 1963, No. 30956 had the same fate in January 1963.
Photo taken on 27th January 1954 by Dick Sansbury

The crew of '0395' 0-6-0 No. 30566 are lucky to be in the warmest place in this wintry view at the front of Eastleigh shed. The engine is fitted with a snowplough and is on snow clearance duties. Behind her can be seen the large water tank and water treatment tower. No. 30566 was built by Neilson of Glasgow; their works number 3459 in December 1885. Her London and South Western number was 101. She cost £2,395 to build. Her end came when she was broken up at Eastleigh in April 1959. Photo taken on 3rd February 1954 by Dick Sansbury

'King Arthur' Class No. 30747 *Elaine* would more appropriately be named The Ice Maiden in this view. She stands out of use at the back of Eastleigh shed. She was built as one of Robert Urie's 'N15' Class at Eastleigh in July 1922. Richard Maunsell rebuilt her at her birthplace in November 1930. She was withdrawn in October 1956 and also broken up at Eastleigh. Photo taken on 27th January 1954 by Dick Sansbury

'Britannia' Pacific No. 70004 *William Shakespeare* stands in spotless condition outside Eastleigh Locomotive Shed. Built at Crewe during March 1951, *William Shakespeare* was given a special finish for exhibition at The Festival of Britain held that year. The Southern Region kept the locomotive at Stewarts Lane depot for the prestigious 'Golden Arrow 'duties. Withdrawn in December 1967 and broken up at Thomas Ward's Inverkeithing.
Photo taken on 3rd August 1954 by Dick Sansbury

The reason for *William Shakespeare*'s appearance at Eastleigh was to be at the open day there, and is seen at the head of a line of engines in this photograph. Immediately behind is a Class '4' Standard 2-6-0 and an LMS 2-6-4 tank. Bulleid 'Merchant Navy' Class No. 35017 *Belgian Marine* heads the left hand line up in front of a 'Battle of Britain' and preserved 'T3' 4-4-0 No. 563, *Ironside* No. 30458 and London Brighton and South Coast 'Terrier '*Boxhill*. The impressive building in the background is the works manager's office and general administrative offices. *Belgian Marine* was built at Eastleigh in April 1945 and rebuilt there in March 1957. On the 22nd October 1945 she was named at Victoria Station by the Belgian Minister of Communications. Withdrawal came in July 1966 after running 1,017,754 miles. She was broken up at Buttigiegs of Newport in September 1966. Photo taken on 4th August 1954 by Dick Sansbury.

The heart of the works was the Erecting Shop and in all its smoky glory Drummond 'M7' 0-4-4 tank No. 30252 awaits overhaul. In the foreground are a pair of diesel bogies from either LMS 10000 or 10001. No. 30252 was built at Nine Elms Works in June 1897 and was withdrawn in February 1959 and broken up at Eastleigh a month later. Photo taken on 4th August 1954 by Dick Sansbury.

A photograph showing a real works environment during the heydays of the 1950s. Bulleid 'West Country' Pacific No. 34026 *Yes Tor* is being worked on in the Erecting Shop. Some of the cladding has been removed revealing the well-liked and free-steaming Bulleid boiler. *Yes Tor* was built at Brighton in April 1946 and rebuilt at Eastleigh in February 1958. Withdrawal came in September 1966 after running 916,244 miles. She was broken up at Buttigiegs of Newport. Photo taken on 4th August 1954 by Dick Sansbury

A product of Nine Elms works is seen being overhauled at the LSWR's new works. Drummond 'M7' 0-4-4 tank No. 30110 is surrounded by various parts of locomotives. The Westinghouse pump on her smokebox side is for operating the Southern's push pull stock. She was built at Nine Elms works in March 1904 and withdrawn and broken up at Eastleigh during May 1963.
Photo taken on 4th August 1954 by Dick Sansbury

Maunsell's 'Lord Nelson' class No. 30855 *Robert Blake* is the centre of attention. The locomotive is wheel-less with the chassis being propped up by bottle jacks and baulks of timber. No hard hats on here, in fact a modern day health and safety inspector would have nightmares! *Robert Blake* was built at Eastleigh in November 1928, withdrawn in September 1961 and broken up at Eastleigh works in February 1962. Photo taken on 4th August 1954 by Dick Sansbury.

A Bulleid Pacific's frames are being worked on in this picture. A locomotive would be stripped down and the various component parts would be sent to the appropriate 'shops' in the works. The two white lines were supposed to be kept clear, so that materials and workmen could pass safely by, which is obviously not the case here! Photo taken on 4th August 1954 by Dick Sansbury

The Vaughan Crane Company of Manchester's overhead crane could lift 50 tons, and has lifted Standard class '4' 2-6-4 tank No. 80012 from her wheels. 'Merchant Navy' Class No. 35005 *Canadian Pacific* and a 'Schools' Class 4-4-0 can be seen in the background. No. 80012 was built at Brighton in September 1951 and was withdrawn in March 1967. She was broken up at Buttigiegs, Newport in September 1967. Photo taken on 4th August 1954 by Dick Sansbury

A boiler from a Maunsell 4-6-0, either a 'King Arthur', 'S15' or 'H15' locomotive waits to be taken to the boiler shop. The tubes in front of the Bulleid Pacific are superheater elements. The white lined pathway has no obstructions on it here! Photo taken on 4th August 1954 by Dick Sansbury

The noisiest place in the works was the boiler shop, and the boiler smiths had no ear protection in those days. Most would become deafer as they got older. A boiler barrel is being riveted in this picture. Bulleid introduced welded steel fireboxes for his Pacifics. Photo taken on 4th August 1954 by Dick Sansbury.

Urie 'HI5' 4-6-0 No. 30483 waits to depart Eastleigh station. The locomotive disc code states that the train is for Southampton Terminus. Eastleigh station's 'up' platform and covered footbridge are still recognisable today, but the 'down' platform has been rebuilt. The Hants and Dorset buses and their depot at the left of the picture have disappeared. No. 30483 was built at Eastleigh in March 1914 and was fitted with a Maunsell superheater in September 1929. Withdrawal and breaking up at Eastleigh came during June 1957. Photo taken 10th March 1956 by Dick Sansbury.

Bulleid 'Merchant Navy' class No. 35004 *Cunard White Star* is seen in ex-works condition and newly rebuilt at Eastleigh. She was originally built at Eastleigh in October 1941 and was rebuilt there in June/July 1958. On The 1st January 1942 Sir P E Bates, chairman of Cunard White Star Line, named her at Charing Cross Station. Withdrawal came in October 1965 after running 1,131,417 miles. She was broken up at Eastleigh by George Cohen's in February 1966. Photo taken on 8th July 1958 by Dick Sansbury.

Brighton 'Atlantic' No. 32424 *Beachy Head* in a clean condition reposes at the rear of Eastleigh. This beautiful machine was designed by Douglas Earle Marsh for the London Brighton and South Coast Railway, and was built at their Brighton works in September 1911. After running 1,090,661 miles *Beachy Head* was withdrawn in April 1958. She was broken up at Eastleigh a few days after this picture was taken. The Bluebell Railway has plans to build a replica 'Atlantic'. Photo taken on 30th April 1958 by Dick Sansbury.

Maunsell 'King Arthur' 4-6-0 No. 30451 *Sir Lamorak* stands at the back of Eastleigh shed in immaculate ex-works condition. The beautiful lines of the 'King Arthurs' can be clearly seen here. *Sir Lamorak* was built at Eastleigh in June 1925, withdrawn in June 1962 and broken up at Eastleigh. Photo by George Wheeler (Collection of Barry J Eagles).

Above: DS35 the Eastleigh 36 ton breakdown crane stands outside the shed. This crane had been built by Ransom and Rapier of Ipswich for the London and South Western Railway in 1917. It came to Eastleigh in 1946 from Fratton, and was used at Eastleigh until 1964 as part of the breakdown train. The USA 0-6-0 tank No. 30073 was built by Vulcan Ironworks USA in 1943 bought by the Southern Railway in June 1947 for shunting in Southampton Docks. Withdrawal came in December 1966, broken up by Cashmores Newport in June 1967. Photo by Dick Sansbury.

Left: One of Bulleid's unconventional but powerful 'Q1' 0-6-0s, No. 33023, is being coaled at the rear of Eastleigh shed. The roofs and chimney tops of the railway houses in Campbell Road can be seen. 33023 was built at Ashford in June 1942. She was withdrawn in June 1964 and broken up by Kings's of Norwich six months later. Photo taken on 11th October 1958 by Dick Sansbury. 23 23

Adams '02' 0-4-4 tank No. 30192 in ex-works condition at the rear of Eastleigh shed. The backs of the railway houses in Campbell Road can be clearly seen. No. 30192 was built at Nine Elms Works in November 1890, one of a class of 60. Twenty-three were sent to the Isle of Wight. Withdrawal came in August 1961, broken up at Eastleigh a month later. Photo by George Wheeler (Collection of Barry J Eagles).

Urie 'H15' 4-6-0 No. 30488 ex-works at Eastleigh where she was built in April 1914. This view shows the spectacle available to a photographer when a locomotive was outshopped from a major overhaul. These mixed traffic engines were Urie's first design for the London and South Western Railway and were solidly built and everything was easily accessible. Withdrawn in April 1959 and broken up at Eastleigh a month later.
Photo by George Wheeler (Collection of Barry J Eagles).

Drummond 'T9' 4-4-0 No. 30337 stands at the back of Eastleigh shed after just completing a running-in turn. She was built at the Nine Elms Works in September 1901 and fitted with a Urie superheated boiler in May 1925, 30337 was one of 66 'Greyhounds'. Withdrawal came in December 1958. Broken up at Eastleigh in January 1959. Photo by George Wheeler (Collection of Barry J Eagles).

Adams '0415' 4-4-2 tank No. 30583 is posed ex-works in Eastleigh works yard. This Adams 'Radial' tank was built by Neilsons of Glasgow works number 3209 in March 1885 as London and South Western No. 488 - she cost £2,580. Sold in 1917 to the Ministry of Munitions for £2,104 for work at a salvage depot near Sittingbourne, her stay here was short-lived, as she was sold to the East Kent Railway for £900 in April 1919. In 1946 the Southern Railway purchased her for £800 for use on the Lyme Regis branch. Finally withdrawn in July 1961 and happily purchased for preservation by the Bluebell Railway. Photo by George Wheeler (Collection of Barry J Eagles).

One of Maunsell's finest. Here is 'Schools' 4-4-0 No. 30905 *Tonbridge* standing in front of Eastleigh shed's water treatment tower. No. 30905 was one of 40 'Schools' built at Eastleigh, being constructed in May 1930. They were originally built for the Hastings line, which had narrow tunnels. In August 1958 she was paired with the solitary self-trimming tender. Withdrawn in December 1961 and broken up at Eastleigh works two months later.
Photo by George Wheeler (collection of Barry J Eagles).

Maunsell 'King Arthur' 4-6-0 No. 30788 *Sir Urre of the Mount*, gleams at the front of Eastleigh locomotive shed. No. 30788 was one of the 'Scotch' Arthurs, having been built by the North British Locomotive Works of Glasgow, their works number 23284 in September 1925. No. 30788's early days had been spent at Exmouth Junction shed, but latterly it was shedded at Eastleigh and withdrawn in January 1962. It was broken up at Ashford works one month later - the only Scotchman broken up there. Photo by George Wheeler (collection of Barry J Eagles).

Drummond '700' 0-6-0 No. 30309 stands waiting to be uncoupled from the Southern Counties Touring Society's 'South Western Limited' at Eastleigh Station. The '700' class were known as 'Black Motors' by 'South Western locomotive men. No. 30309 was originally London and South Western Railway No. 704. She was built by Dubs of Glasgow their works number 3527 in May 1897 at a cost of £2,695. A superheated boiler was fitted in January 1925. Withdrawn in December 1962 and broken up at Eastleigh in July 1963. The man in the guards uniform to the right of the engine is Mr W E Crawforth, the helpful secretary of the Southern Counties Touring Society. Photo taken on 2nd September 1962 by Barry J Eagles.

Maunsell 'Lord Nelson' 4-6-0 No. 30856 *Lord St Vincent* poses ex-works at Eastleigh; one of 16 'Lord Nelsons'. All were built there, No. 30856 in November 1928 at a cost of £10,150. Sent new to Nine Elms shed, modified by Bulleid with a Lemaitre multiple blastpipe and large diameter chimney in November 1938. Withdrawn from Eastleigh shed in September 1962 and broken up at Eastleigh works two months later.
Photo by George Wheeler (collection of Barry J Eagles).

Bulleid 'Battle of Britain' No. 34051 *Winston Churchill* stands ex-works at Eastleigh shed. Built at Brighton works in December 1946 and allocated to Salisbury shed. Its finest hour came in January 1965, when it hauled it namesake's funeral train from Waterloo to Oxfordshire. Withdrawal came in September 1965 after running 807,496 miles. The locomotive is now preserved as part of the National Collection. Photo by George Wheeler (collection of Barry J Eagles).

Standard class '5' 4-6-0 No. 73049 stands in Eastleigh works yard after overhaul. She was built at Derby works in December 1953, one of 130 built there. 42 were built at Doncaster works. She was stationed at Bath, Somerset and Dorset shed for much of her early life. Withdrawn from Oxford shed in March 1965 and broken up by Birds of Risca three months later. Photo by George Wheeler (collection of Barry J Eagles).

Maunsell 'N' 2-6-0 No. 31816 is ex-works and awaiting duties at the rear of Eastleigh shed. Maunsell's 'Moguls' were the workhorses of the Southern and could be seen from Padstow to Dover. Originally one of Maunsell's designs for the South Eastern and Chatham Railway, the first South Eastern and Chatham No. 810 was built at Ashford in July 1917. No. 31816 was built at Ashford at a cost of £5,875 in December 1921 and withdrawn in January 1966, she was broken up by Cashmores of Newport in April 1966. Photo taken on 24th February 1963 by Barry J Eagles.

Longmoor Military Railway 2-10-0 No. WD601 *Kitchener* ex-works in the locomotive works yard. These locomotives were designed by RA Riddles. *Kitchener* was at first numbered WD73797 and was built at the North British Locomotive Company of Glasgow; their works number 25643, in August 1945. It was retained by the War Department after the Second World War at Longmoor and worked there until withdrawal in 1967. 150 of these machines were built at a cost of £12,500 each. Photo by George Wheeler (collection of Barry J Eagles).

Drummond '700' class 0-6-0 No. 30316 looks a weary work-stained workhorse, as she stands outside the front of Eastleigh shed attached to a snowplough. Modern diesel and electric traction can be seen on the right. No. 30316, one of the 30 strong '700' class, was originally London and South Western Railway No. 716. She was built by Dubs of Glasgow (their works number 3539) in June 1897; a superheated boiler was fitted by Urie in December 1920. In her later days she was allocated to Eastleigh shed for working local goods. It was withdrawn in December 1962 and broken up at Eastleigh in May 1963.
Photo taken on 24th February 1963 by Barry J Eagles

Maunsell 'H15' 4-6-0 No. 30522 slumbers in the autumn sun at the rear of Eastleigh shed. No. 30522 was built at Eastleigh in July 1924. A Maunsell superheater was fitted in April 1929. The 'H15' class consisted of 26 engines, ten had been built by Urie, ten by Maunsell. Five locomotives had been rebuilt from Drummond class 'F13', and one from the Drummond 'E14' class. No. 30522 was withdrawn in October 1961 and broken up a month later at Eastleigh works. Photo taken on 23rd September 1961 by Barry J Eagles.

Stroudley 'A1' 0-6-0 tank No. DS680 heads a line-up of engines at Eastleigh on a Sunday afternoon, a locospotter's paradise, as engines are lit up for the week's work ahead. No. DS680 had a long and interesting career. Built at Brighton in February 1876 as London, Brighton and South Coast Railway No. 54 and named *Waddon*. Sold in August 1904 for £670 to the South Eastern and Chatham Railway and renumbered 751, it became the Lancing works shunter in 1932 with the number 680S and remaining there until withdrawal in June 1962 with the number DS680. Presented to the Canadian Historical Association and after restoration shipped to Canada where she now resides. Photo taken on 24th February 1963 by Barry J Eagles.

Urie 'S15' 4-6-0 No. 30500 catches the wintry afternoon sunlight at the rear of Eastleigh shed. The 'S15s' were Urie's third and final class of 4-6-0s. They were basically a goods version of the 'N15' class. No. 30500 was built at Eastleigh in May 1920 at a cost of £9,512. A Maunsell superheater was fitted in October 1930. She was withdrawn in June 1963 and broken up at Eastleigh in October 1963. Two Urie 'S15s' still remain to this day courtesy of Woodham's yard at Barry - Nos. 30499 and 30506 owned by the Urie Locomotive Society. Photo taken on 14th February 1963 by Barry J Eagles.

Bulleid 'coffeepot' 'Q1' 0-6-0 No. 33021 runs light engine through Eastleigh station. The headcode is correct for it is the one for light engines from Basingstoke to Eastleigh. No. 33021 was one of the 40 strong 'Q1' class built at Ashford in June 1942 and withdrawn in August 1963 and broken up at Eastleigh in October 1963. Photo taken on 31st of March 1963 by Barry J Eagles.

Urie 'H16' class 4-6-2 tank No. 30517 shows its massive contours at the rear of Eastleigh shed. One of a class of five built for transfer goods from Feltham Yard, No. 30517 was built at Eastleigh in November 1921 and was shedded at Feltham for most of her life. Withdrawal came in November 1962 with breaking up at Eastleigh in June 1963. Photo taken on 24th February 1963 by Barry J Eagles.

Adams '02' 0-4-4 tank No. 30225 stands in the scrap road at Eastleigh. Built for working suburban services and branch line work for the London and South Western Railway. No. 30225 was built at Nine Elms at a cost of £1,500 in November 1892 - her final duty was station pilot at Eastleigh. Withdrawal came in December 1962 and was broken up at Eastleigh in May 1963. Photo taken on 7th April 1963 by Barry J Eagles.

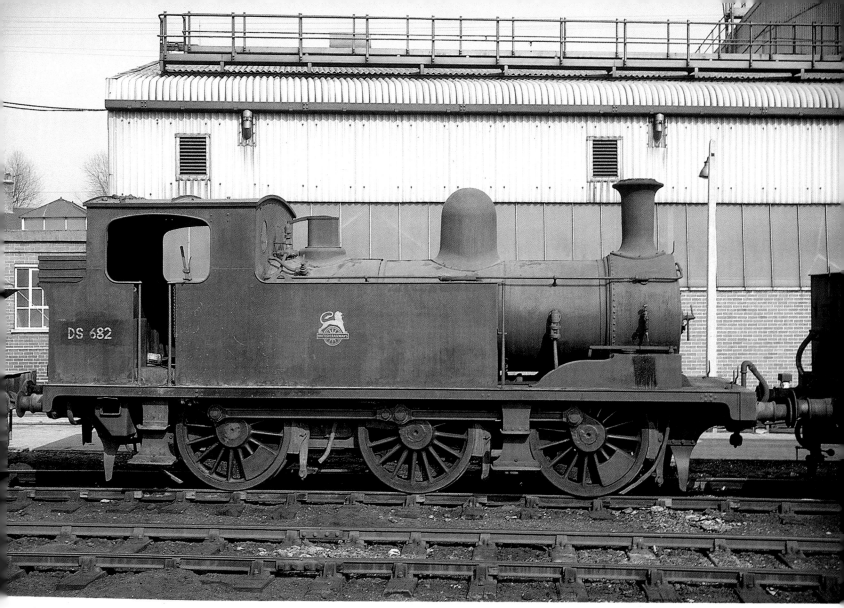

Adams 'G6' 0-6-0 tank No. DS682. The last survivor of her class waits to be broken up at Eastleigh. One of a class of 34 engines, No. DS682 was built at Nine Elms Works in September 1898 as No. 238, at a cost of £1,150. This low cost was achieved due to No. 238 having a second-hand boiler from Beattie Well Tank No. 0189. In November 1960 she was transferred to Meldon Quarry and renumbered DS682 in service stock. Withdrawn in December 1962 and broken up at Eastleigh in May 1963. Photo taken on 7th April 1963 by Barry J Eagles.

Drummond 'M7' 0-4-4 tank No. 30105 at the rear of Eastleigh shed shows her elegant lines. One of a class of 105 engines, 95 of which were built at Nine Elms Works and 10 at Eastleigh. No. 30105 was built at Nine Elms Works in March 1905 at a cost of £1,445. She was withdrawn in May 1963 from Bournemouth shed and broken up at Eastleigh in June 1963. Two 'M7s' are preserved; No.s 30053 and 30245. Photo taken on 7th April 1963 by Barry J Eagles.

Bulleid 'Q1' 0-6-0 No. 33020 is in the last stages of an overhaul at Eastleigh Works. Her austere lines can be clearly seen. These powerful goods engines greatly helped the extremely busy Southern Railway during the Second World War. It was built at Ashford in May 1942, one of the twenty of the class built there. The other twenty were built in Brighton. Withdrawn in January 1966 and broken up at Buttigiegs in Newport, the first of the class number 33001 is preserved in the National Collection. Photo taken on 21st April 1963 by Barry J Eagles.

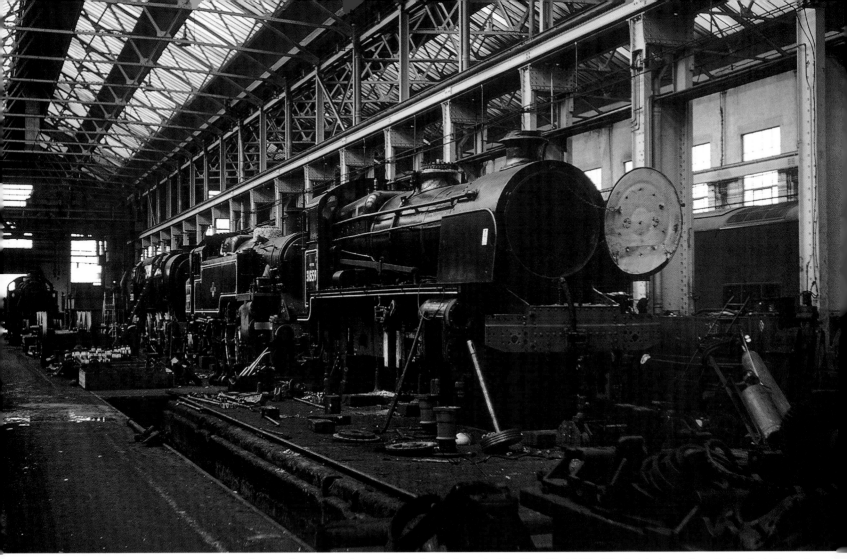

Maunsell 'N' 2-6-0 No. 31859 under overhaul in the erecting shop at Eastleigh. At the end of the First World War, Woolwich Arsenal needed to find alternative employment for its workforce. Ashford Works of the South Eastern and Chatham Railway supplied the Arsenal with drawings of the 'Ns'. Boilers were built by the North British Locomotive Company of Glasgow (76), Robert Stephenson of Newcastle (20) and Kitson of Leeds (14). These boilers were sent to Woolwich so that they could build 100 locomotives, with 10 spare boilers. The Southern Railway bought 50 of these handy engines at the bargain price of £3,962 each, henceforth their nickname became Woolworths. 27 sets of parts went to Ireland and 6 sets to the Metropolitan Railway. The remaining boilers and spares were bought by the Southern and incorporated in other classes of engines. No. 31859 was built at Woolwich in April 1925, and withdrawn in September 1964, and broken up at Birds Commercial Motors Morriston. No. 31874 has been preserved. Photo taken on 21st April 1963 by Barry J Eagles.

An avenue of steam locomotives leads to an electro-diesel. On the left are Bulleid Pacifics with their distinctive smokebox doors and on the right two Maunsell Moguls hide behind standard class '4' 2-6-4 tank No. 80138 built at Brighton in June 1956. Withdrawal came in December 1966, being broken up at Cashmores Newport in February 1967. Photo taken on 21st April 1963 by Barry J Eagles.

Maunsell 'S15' 4-6-0 No. 30828 stands out of use at the rear of Eastleigh shed. After Urie had built 20 of his 'S15' class, Maunsell improved the design and built a further 25. No. 30828 was one of those. Built at Eastleigh in July 1927, she was withdrawn in January 1964 and sold to Woodhams of Barry. She languished there until bought by the Eastleigh Railway Preservation Society and returned to working order at Eastleigh works. Nos. 30825, 30830, 30841 and 30847 survived their sojourn at the Barry yard and have been preserved. Photo taken on 28th April 1963 by Barry J Eagles.

Maunsell 'N' 2-6-0 No. 31831 at the rear of Eastleigh shed, one of the 'Woolworths'. No. 31831 was built at Woolwich in June 1924. In August 1960 it was fitted with a BR standard class '4' chimney and blast pipe. Withdrawal came in April 1965 and she was broken up by Cashmores of Newport. Photo taken on 5th May 1963 by Barry J Eagles.

Maunsell 'S15' 4-6-0 No. 30837 stands alongside Eastleigh shed's coal stage. Built at Eastleigh in January 1928, No. 30837 was sent to Feltham shed and withdrawn from that shed in September 1965 to be broken up a year later by Cashmores of Newport. It was the last 'S15' used in service on BR.
Photo taken on 5th May 1963 by Barry J Eagles.

USA 0-6-0 tank No. DS236 is ex-works at Eastleigh shed. It is waiting to take up its duties at Lancing Carriage Works. DS236 was built at the Vulcan Iron Works of Wilkes-Barre, Pennsylvania, USA, their works number 4488 of 1943, for the United States Army Transportation Corp. The Southern Railway was looking for shunting locomotives for Southampton Docks and bought 14 of the class, plus one for spare from the Newbury Racecourse dump at a cost of £2,500 each. DS236 was numbered 30074 until April 1963. This locomotive was the first of the class to be taken into stock in May 1946 and used on trials in Southampton Docks. Withdrawn in June 1965 and broken up at Eastleigh by George Cohen. Photo taken on 5th May 1963 by Barry J Eagles.

Above: Bulleid 'Battle of Britain' No. 34057 *Biggin Hill* stands at the rear of Eastleigh shed. Built at Brighton works in March 1947 and allocated to Stewarts Lane shed it was named after the famous Second World War airbase. No. 34057 was one of the last Unrebuilt Bulleids to survive before the end of steam in 1967 and was withdrawn in the May after running 939,597 miles. Broken up at Cashmores, Newport in October 1967.
Photo taken on 5th May 1963 by Barry J Eagles.

Right: Drummond '700' 0-6-0 No. 30309 is caught in the evening sunlight at Eastleigh shed. One of 30 'black motors', No. 30309's full details are on page number 30. Photo taken on 2nd June 1963 by Barry J Eagles.

Maunsell 'W' 2-6-4 tank No. 31921 at Eastleigh shed. One of a class of 15 three-cylinder tank engines, No. 31921 was built at Ashford works in October 1935, at a cost of £9,210. 10 were built at Ashford and five at Eastleigh. Used mainly on cross London goods, No. 31921 was withdrawn from Norwood Junction in June 1963 and broken up at Eastleigh in October 1963. Photo taken on 16th June 1963 by Barry J Eagles.

Maunsell 'Schools' 4-4-0 No. 30934 *St Lawrence*, stands awaiting the cutters' torch at the rear of Eastleigh works. No. 30934 was built at Eastleigh in March 1935. Bulleid fitted a large diameter chimney and a Lemaitre blast pipe in May 1940. Withdrawn in December 1962 No. 30934 steamed to Eastleigh on the 18th May 1963, where she was broken up in August 1963. Photo taken on 7th August 1963 by Barry J Eagles.

'West Country' No. 34033 *Chard* heads a line-up of engines at Eastleigh coaling stage. Built at Brighton Works in July 1946 and allocated to Stewarts Lane Shed, she was withdrawn in December 1965 after running 884,916 miles and broken up at Buttigiegs Newport in May 1966.
Photo taken on 28th July 1963 by Barry J Eagles.

Maunsell 'N1' 2-6-0 No. 31877 stands by the water tank and dormitory at Eastleigh shed. The sighting test signal can be clearly seen. One of a class of six three-cylinder engines, No. 31877 was built at Ashford Works in April 1930 at a cost of £8.940. Withdrawn along with the other five class members in November 1962 after running 762,536 miles it was broken up at Eastleigh in August 1963. Photo taken on 28th July 1963 by Barry J Eagles.

The storm clouds gather behind Billington 'E4' 0-6-2 tank No. 32557. This locomotive was originally numbered 557 and named *Northlands*, and was built at Brighton in September 1901 for the London Brighton and South Coast Railway. Known as the large radials, there were 75 members of the class all built at Brighton. Withdrawn in December 1962 from Nine Elms Shed and broken up at Eastleigh in October 1963. No. 473 *Birch Grove* has been preserved at the Bluebell Railway. Photo taken on 12th September 1963 by Barry J Eagles.

Drummond '700' class 0-6-0 No. 30697 waits for the worst as it catches the wintry sun on the scrap road at Eastleigh shed. She was built by Dubs of Glasgow, their works number 3520 in April 1897. A superheated boiler was fitted to Urie's design in September 1925. Withdrawn from Exmouth Junction shed in November 1962, but not broken up until March 1964 at Eastleigh. No. 30368 of the class was offered to the Hampshire Railfans Club for £1.075! Photo taken on 26th January 1964 by Barry J Eagles.

Adams '02' 0-4-4 tank No. 30199 looks very weather stained at Eastleigh. She was built at Nine Elms in June 1891 and withdrawn in December 1962. Broken up at Eastleigh a year later after an unsuccessful attempt by the Hampshire Railfans Club to purchase her for £700!
Photo taken on 13th September 1963 by Barry J Eagles.

Gresley 'A3' No. 4472 *Flying Scotsman* stands at the entrance to Eastleigh shed after working a Railfans Special. The well-travelled *Flying Scotsman* was withdrawn from British Railways as No. 60103 in January 1963 and is still in steam today. Class '4' 2-6-0 No. 76063 was built at Doncaster in July 1956 the same works as *Flying Scotsman*. Withdrawal came in April 1967 and it was broken up by Buttigiegs, Newport.
Photo taken on 16th August 1964 by Barry J Eagles.

USA 0-6-0 tank No. 30072 is spotless as she shunts Eastleigh works. She was built by the Vulcan Iron Works of Wilkes-Barre, Pennsylvania, USA. Their works number 4446 of 1943, for the United States Army Transportation Corp. Her War Department number was WD 1973. Bought from Newbury Race Course Dump for the bargain price of £2,500. 30072 entered service in April 1947 and was withdrawn in July 1967 and sold for preservation on the Keighley Worth Valley Railway. Photo taken on 17th September 1964 by Barry J Eagles.

Maunsell 'Q' 0-6-0 No. 30548 poses at the rear of Eastleigh shed. It was one of twenty of the class built at Eastleigh. No. 30548 was built there in March 1939. In November 1948 Bulleid had it fitted with a Lemaitre blastpipe and a large diameter chimney. Withdrawn in March 1965 and broken up four months later at Cox and Danks, Park Royal. No. 30541 has been preserved by the Maunsell Locomotive Society. Photo taken on 17th of September 1964 by Barry J Eagles.

Adams 'B4' 0-4-0 tank No. 30102 and Stroudley 'AIX' No. 32662 stand beautifully restored outside Eastleigh works. Both had been bought for display by Butlins holiday camps. No. 30102 was built at Nine Elms in December 1893. In April 1896 it was transferred to Southampton Docks and named *Granville*. Withdrawn in September 1963. One other member of the class, No. 30096, is preserved. No. 32662 was built at Brighton Works at a cost of £1,800 in October 1875 and named *Martello* and rebuilt to class 'AIX' in December 1912; it was withdrawn in November 1963 and preserved along with several others. Photo taken on 17th September 1964 by Barry J Eagles.

Drummond 'M7' 0-4-4 tank No. 30133 at the rear of Eastleigh shed. No. 30133 clearly shows the Westinghouse pump, air tanks and plumbing needed to operate the Southern's push-pull system. She was built at Nine Elms works in March 1903 but was not push-pull fitted until 1960. Withdrawn in March 1964 after running 1,816,324 miles, No. 30133 was not broken up until November 1965 at Cashmores, Newport, South Wales. Her boiler was going to be used to restore Highland Railway, *Ben Alder* to working order but this unfortunately was not to be and *Ben Alder* was broken up too.
Photo taken on 17th September 1964 by Barry J Eagles.

Above: Standard Class '4' 2-6-4 tank No. 80068 departs from Eastleigh shed, the housing in Southampton Road in the background can be clearly seen. No. 80068 was built at Brighton in September 1953, one of a class of 155 engines. 130 were built in Brighton, 15 in Derby and 10 in Doncaster. The first years of her life were spent on the London Midland Region until transfer in 1959 to Stewarts Lane on the Southern. Withdrawal came in October 1966 and breaking up at Cashmores, Newport in February 1967. Nos. 80002, 80064, 80072, 80078, 80079, 80080, 80097, 80098, 80100, 80104, 80105, 80135, 80136, 80150 and 80151 are all preserved. Photo taken on 28th March 1965 by Barry J Eagles.

Right: USA 0-6-0 No. 30071 undertakes shed pilot duties at Eastleigh shed. She was built by the Vulcan Iron Works of Wilkes-Barre, Pennsylvania, USA. Their works number 4439 of 1943, for the United States Army Transportation Corp. Her War Department number was WD1966. 30071 entered service in November 1947 and was withdrawn in July 1967 and broken up at Cashmores, Newport in March 1968. Nos. 30064, 30065, 30070 and 30072 have all been preserved. Photo taken on 28th March 1965 by Barry J Eagles.

66

'West Country' Pacific No. 34102 *Lapford* stands by Eastleigh's coaling stage, after working a Union Castle Line Boat Train. One of the six 'West Country's' built at Eastleigh, No. 34102 was completed there in February 1950 and allocated to Stewarts Lane shed. Withdrawn in July 1967 after running 593,438 miles and having the distinction of being the last unrebuilt Bulleid Pacific to operate on the Southern Region. It was broken up at Buttigiegs, Newport in September 1968. Photo taken on 3rd June 1965 by Barry J Eagles.

Another 'West Country' Pacific, No. 34004 *Yeovil,* stands by Eastleigh coaling stage after working a Cunard Boat Train. Built at Brighton works in July 1945 and allocated to Exmouth Junction shed, she was rebuilt at Eastleigh in February 1958. Withdrawn in July 1967 after running 920,972 miles and broken up at Cashmores, Newport in October 1967. Ten original and ten rebuilt engines are preserved. Photo taken on 3rd June 1965 by Barry J Eagles.

London Transport 0-6-0 pannier tank L90 has just arrived from the London Transport Depot at Neasden. L90 was built by the North British Locomotive Company of Glasgow; their works number 24048 for the Great Western Railway as No. 7760. In January 1962 it was sold to London Transport and withdrawn in June 1971 and preserved. It was overhauled by Eastleigh works in exchange for the loan of a mobile rail welding machine used on the Bournemouth Electrification. Photo taken on 18th September 1965 by D M Cox

Two locomotives from the 1940s and 1950s show their front ends at Eastleigh MPD. 'Q1' 0-6-0 No. 33027 and Standard Class '4' 4-6-0 No. 75066 lurk in the stygian gloom of Eastleigh shed. No. 33027 was built at Brighton works in July 1942 and withdrawn in January 1966. She was broken up at Buttigiegs, Newport. No. 75066 was built at Swindon in September 1955, one of a class of 80 locomotives. Withdrawal came in January 1966 and breaking up at Cashmores, Newport during April 1966. Nos. 75014, 75027, 75029, 75069, 75078 and 75079 are preserved. Photo taken on 17th October 1965 by Barry J Eagles.

Gresley 'A4' Pacific No. 60024 *Kingfisher* takes on coal at Eastleigh after working a special train for the A4 Preservation Society. She was built at the Doncaster Works of the London and North Eastern Railway in December 1936 and numbered 4483. *Kingfisher* worked many specials in her latter days. No. 60024 was withdrawn in September 1966, and broken up by Hughes Bolckows Ltd at North Blyth. Nos. 60007, 60008, 60009, 60010, 60019 and 60022 are preserved. Photo taken on 26th March 1966 by Barry J Eagles.

Earlier that year, in the January, 'S15' 4-6-0 No. 30837 is as shiny as a new pin as she stands at the front of Eastleigh shed. It has just worked the Locomotive Club of Great Britain's 'S15 Commemorative Rail Tour'. She was built at Eastleigh in January 1928 and withdrawn in September 1965, but reinstated to work the special. Photo taken on 9th January 1966 by Barry J Eagles.

Maunsell 'U' 2-6-0 No. 31639 stands by the water tank and dormitory at Eastleigh shed. No. 31639 was built at Ashford in May 1931, the last built member of the 50-strong class. Originally designed as the 'K' class 2-6-4 tank for the South Eastern and Chatham Railway in July 1917, twenty were built and named after south of England rivers. Owing to complaints of rough riding and a derailment at Sevenoaks on the 24th August 1927, they were converted to 2-6-0 tender locomotives and became very useful engines. No. 31639 was withdrawn in June 1966 and broken up at Cashmores, Newport in September 1966. Numbers 31618, 31625, 31638 and 31806 are preserved. Photo taken on 16th January 1966 by Barry J Eagles.

Drummond 'T9' No. 120 poses in Eastleigh Works Yard prior to an open day in 1992. This preserved graceful-looking 'Greyhound' was built at Nine Elms Works in August 1899. A superheater was fitted in May 1927. At the end of 1961 No. 30120 was selected for preservation and overhauled at Eastleigh Works. This was completed on 10th March 1962 as London and South Western Railway No. 120. Over the next couple of years she worked many enthusiasts specials. Now part of the National Collection, No. 120 is awaiting overhaul at the Bluebell Railway after successfully being restored to working order again by the Urie Locomotive Society in 1983. Photo taken on 26th September 1992 by Barry J Eagles.

Eastleigh's pride and joy - Maunsell 'S15' 4-6-0 No. E828 stands in the evening sunlight with Bulleid 'West Country' Pacific No. 34027 *Taw Valley* in the background in the works yard. E828 has been based on the Swanage Railway in recent times. *Taw Valley* was built at Brighton in April 1946 and was allocated to Ramsgate Shed. She was rebuilt at Eastleigh in September 1957. Withdrawn in August 1964, after running 764,316 miles, she made her way to Woodhams Yard at Barry. *Taw Valley* was bought for preservation after 15 years in the yard and has been restored to main line working order.
Photo taken on 26th September 1992 by Barry J Eagles.

Drummond 'M7' 0-4-4 tank No. 30053 is coupled to a 'Queen Mary' Bogie Brake van at Eastleigh Works. No. 30053 was one of a class of 105 engines and was built at Nine Elms Works in December 1905. She was withdrawn in May 1964, but reinstated to work a rail tour on the 5th July 1964. No. 30053 was bought by the Steam Town Foundation of Bellow Falls, Vermont, USA, and after a cosmetic restoration was shipped there. She was never steamed in her sojourn in the USA, and was bought by the Drummond Locomotive Society and repatriated to England. Restored to working order, No. 30053 now resides at the Swanage Railway. Photo taken on 26th September 1992 by Barry J Eagles.

List of Steam Locomotives Built or Rebuilt at Eastleigh

LSWR SR	British Rail	Building Date			LSWR SR	British Rail	Building Date	Name		LSWR SR	British Rail	Building Date	
DRUMMOND CLASS 'S14', 0-4-0T					**URIE CLASS 'H15', 4-6-0**					**URIE CLASS 'G16', 4-8-0T**			
101		Sep. 1910			486	30486	Jan. 1914			492	30492	Jul. 1921	
147		Sep. 1910			487	30487	Feb. 1914			493	30493	Jul. 1921	
					482	30482	Mar. 1914			494	30494	Aug. 1921	
DRUMMOND CLASS 'P14', 4-6-0					483	30483	Apr. 1914			495	30495	Aug. 1921	
448		Dec. 1910			488	30488	Apr. 1914						
449		Dec. 1910			484	30484	May 1914			**URIE CLASS 'H16', 4-6-2T**			
450		Jan. 1911			489	30489	Jun. 1914			516	30516	Nov. 1921	
451		Feb. 1911			485	30485	Jun. 1914			517	30517	Nov. 1921	
452		Feb. 1911			490	30490	Jul. 1914			518	30518	Dec. 1921	
					491	30491	Jul. 1914			519	30519	Jan. 1922	
DRUMMOND CLASS 'T14', 4-6-0					335	30335	Jan. 1915			520	30520	Feb. 1922	
443	30443	Apr. 1911											
444	30444	May 1911			**URIE CLASS 'N15', 4-6-0**					**URIE CLASS 'N15', 4-6-0 (cont.)**			
445	30445	Jun. 1911			736	30736	Sep. 1918	*Excalibur*		746	30746	Jun. 1922	*Pendragon*
446	30446	Jul. 1911			737	30737	Oct. 1918	*King Uther*		747	30747	Jul. 1922	*Elaine*
447	30447	Jul. 1911			738	30738	Dec. 1918	*King Pellinore*		748	30748	Aug. 1922	*Vivien*
					739	30739	Feb. 1919	*King Leodegrance*		749	30749	Sep. 1922	*Iseult*
DRUMMOND CLASS 'M7', 0-4-4T					740	30740	Apr. 1919	*Merlin*		750	30750	Oct. 1922	*Morgan le Fay*
125	30125	Aug. 1911			741	30741	May 1919	*Joyous Gard*		751	30751	Nov. 1922	*Etarre*
126		Sep. 1911			742	30742	Jun. 1919	*Camelot*		752	30752	Dec. 1922	*Linette*
127	30127	Oct. 1911			743	30743	Aug. 1919	*Lyonnesse*		753	30753	Jan. 1923	*Melisande*
128	30128	Nov. 1911			744	30744	Sep. 1919	*Maid of Astolat*		754	30754	Feb. 1923	*The Green Knight*
129	30129	Nov. 1911			745	30745	Nov. 1919	*Tintagel*		755	30755	Mar. 1923	*The Red Knight*
131	30131	Nov. 1911											
328	30328	Nov. 1911			**URIE CLASS 'S15', 4-6-0**					**MAUNSELL CLASS 'H15', 4-6-0 (cont.)**			
479	30479	Nov. 1911			497	30497	Mar. 1920			E473	30473	Feb. 1924	
480	30480	Nov. 1911			498	30498	Apr. 1920			E474	30474	Feb. 1924	
481	30481	Nov. 1911			499	30499	May 1920			E475	30475	Mar. 1924	
DRUMMOND CLASS 'T14', 4-6-0 (cont.)					500	30500	May 1920			E476	30476	Apr. 1924	
458		Jan. 1912			501	30501	Jun. 1920			E477	30477	May 1924	
459		Jun. 1912			502	30502	Jul. 1920			E478	30478	Jun. 1924	
460	30460	Feb. 1912			503	30503	Aug. 1920			E521	30521	Jul. 1924	
461	30461	Apr. 1912			504	30504	Sep. 1920			E522	30522	Jul.. 1924	
462	30462	May 1912			505	30505	Oct. 1920			E523	30523	Sep. 1924	
					506	30506	Oct. 1920			E524	30524	Sep. 1924	
DRUMMOND CLASS 'D15', 4-4-0					507	30507	Nov. 1920			E330	30330	Oct. 1924	
463	30463	Apr 1912			508	30508	Dec. 1920			E331	30331	Nov. 1924	
464	30464	May 1912			509	30509	Dec. 1920			E332	30332	Dec. 1924	
465	30465	Jul. 1912			510	30510	Jan. 1921			E333	30333	Dec. 1924	
466	30466	Jul. 1912			511	30511	Jan. 1921			E334	30334	Jan. 1925	
467	30467	Aug. 1912			512	30512	Feb. 1921						
468	30468	Sep. 1912			513	30513	Mar. 1921			**MAUNSELL CLASS 'N15' (cont.)**			
469	30469	Oct. 1912			514	30514	Mar. 1921			E453	30453	Feb. 1925	*King Arthur*
470	30470	Nov. 1912			515	30515	Apr. 1921			E454	30454	Mar. 1925	*Queen Guinevere*
471	30471	Dec. 1912			496	30496	May 1921			E455	30455	Mar. 1925	*Sir Launcelot*
472	30472	Jan. 1913								E456	30456	Apr. 1925	*Sir Galahad*

E457	30457	Apr.	19..	
E448	30448	May	1925	
E449	30449	Jun.	1925	Sir Torre
E450	30450	Jun.	1925	Sir Kay
E451	30451	Jun.	1925	Sir Lamorak
E452	30452	Jul.	1925	Sir Meliagrance
E793	30793	Mar.	1926	Sir Ontzlake
E794	30794	Mar.	1926	Sir Ector de Maris
E795	30795	Apr.	1926	Sir Dinadan
E796	30796	May	1926	Sir Dodinas le Savage
E797	30797	Jun.	1926	Sir Blamore de Ganis
E798	30798	Jun.	1926	Sir Hectimere
E799	30799	Jul.	1926	Sir Ironside

MAUNSELL CLASS 'LN', 4-6-0

E850	30850	Aug.	1926	Lord Nelson

MAUNSELL CLASS 'N15' (cont.)

800	30800	Sep.	1926	Sir Meleaus de Lile
801	30801	Oct.	1926	Sir Meliot de Logres
802	30802	Oct.	1926	Sir Durnore
803	30803	Oct.	1926	Sir Harry le Fise Lake
804	30804	Dec.	1926	Sir Cador of Cornwall
805	30805	Jan.	1927	Sir Constantine
806	30806	Jan.	1927	Sir Galleron

CLASS 'S15' (cont.)

823	30823	Mar.	1927
824	30824	Mar.	1927
825	30825	Apr.	1927
826	30826	May	1927
827	30827	Jun.	1927
828	30828	Jul.	1927
829	30829	Jul.	1927
830	30830	Aug.	1927
831	30831	Sep.	1927
832	30832	Oct.	1927
833	30833	Nov.	1927
834	30834	Nov.	1927
835	30835	Dec.	1927
836	30836	Dec.	1927
837	30837	Jan.	1928

MAUNSELL 'U' CLASS, 2-6-0 (Rebuilt at Eastleigh)

790	31790	Jun.	1928	River Avon
793	31793	Jun.	1928	River Ouse
794	31794	Jun.	1928	River Rother
795	31795	Jun.	1928	River Medway
791	31791	Jul.	1928	River Adur
792	31792	Jul.	1928	River Arun
796	31796	Jul.	1928	River Stour

MAUNSELL 'N15' CLASS, 4-6-0

E851	30851	Jun.	1928	Sir Francis Drake
E852	30852	Jul.	1928	Sir Walter Raleigh
E853	30853	Sep.	1928	Sir Richard Grenville
E854	30854	Oct.	1928	Howard of Effingham
E855	30855	Nov.	1928	Robert Blake
E856	30856	Nov.	1928	Lord St. Vincent
E857	30857	Dec.	1928	Lord Howe
E858	30858	Jan.	1929	Lord Duncan
E859	30859	Mar.	1929	Lord Hood
E860	30860	Apr.	1929	Lord Hawke
E861	30861	Sep.	1929	Lord Anson
E862	30862	Oct.	1929	Lord Collingwood
E863	30863	Oct.	1929	Lord Rodney
E864	30864	Nov.	1929	Sir Martin Frobisher
E865	30865	Nov.	1929	Sir John Hawkins

MAUNSELL CLASS, 'V' 4-4-0

E900	30900	Mar.	1930	Eton
E901	30901	Mar.	1930	Winchester
E902	30902	Apr.	1930	Wellington
E903	30903	Apr.	1930	Charterhouse
E904	30904	May	1930	Lancing
E905	30905	May	1930	Tonbridge
E906	30906	Jun.	1930	Sherborne
E907	30907	Jul.	1930	Dulwich
E908	30908	Jul.	1930	Westminster
E909	30909	Jul.	1930	St. Paul's

MAUNSELL 'U1' CLASS, 2-6-0

A891	31891	Jan.	1931
A892	31892	Jan.	1931
A893	31893	Feb.	1931
A894	31894	Feb.	1931
A895	31895	Mar.	1931
A896	31896	Mar.	1931
A897	31897	Mar.	1931
A898	31898	Apr.	1931
A899	31899	Apr.	1931
A900	31900	May	1931
1901	31901	Jun.	1931
1902	31902	Jul.	1931
1903	31903	Jul.	1931
1904	31904	Jul.	1931
1905	31905	Aug.	1931
1906	31906	Sep.	1931
1907	31907	Sep.	1931
1908	31908	Oct.	1931
1909	31909	Oct.	1931
1910	31910	Nov.	1931

MAUNSELL 'W' CLASS, 2-6-4T

1911	31911	Jan.	1932
1912	31912	Jan.	1932
1913	31913	Jan.	1932
1914	31914	Jan.	1932
1915	31915	Feb.	1932

MAUNSELL CLASS 'V' (cont.)

910	30910	Nov.	1932	Merchant Taylors
911	30911	Dec.	1932	Dover
912	30912	Dec.	1932	Downside
913	30913	Dec.	1932	Christ's Hospital
914	30914	Dec.	1932	Eastbourne
915	30915	May	1933	Brighton
916	30916	May	1933	Whitgift
917	30917	Jun.	1933	Ardingly
918	30918	Jun.	1933	Hurstpierpoint
919	30919	Jun.	1933	Harrow
920	30920	Oct	1933	Rugby
921	30921	Nov.	1933	Shrewsbury
922	30922	Dec.	1933	Marlborough
923	30923	Dec.	1933	Uppingham
924	30924	Dec.	1933	Haileybury
925	30925	Apr.	1934	Cheltenham
926	30926	May	1934	Repton
927	30927	Jun.	1934	Clifton
928	30928	Jun.	1934	Stowe
929	30929	Jul.	1934	Malvern
930	30930	Dec.	1934	Radley
931	30931	Dec.	1934	King's Wimbledon
932	30932	Feb.	1935	Blundell's
933	30933	Feb.	1935	King's Canterbury
934	30934	Mar.	1935	St. Lawrence
935	30935	May	1935	Sevenoaks
936	30936	Jun.	1935	Cranleigh
937	30937	Jun.	1935	Epsom
938	30938	Jul.	1935	St. Olave's
939	30939	Jul.	1935	Leatherhead

'N15X' CLASS, Rebuilt as 4-6-0

2329	32329	Dec.	1934	Stephenson
2327	32327	Apr.	1935	Trevithick
2333	32333	Jun.	1935	Remembrance
2330	32330	Sep.	1935	Cudworth
2332	32332	Nov.	1935	Stroudley
2328	32328	Feb.	1936	Hackworth
2331	32331	Apr.	1936	Beattie

MAUNSELL CLASS 'S15', (cont.)

838	30838	May	1936
839	30839	May	1936
840	30840	Jun.	1936
841	30841	Jul.	1936
842	30842	Aug.	1936
843	30843	Sep.	1936
844	30844	Oct.	1936
845	30845	Oct.	1936
846	30846	Nov.	1936
847	30847	Dec.	1936

MAUNSELL 'Q' CLASS, 0-6-0

SR	British Rail	Building Date	Name
530	30530	Jan. 1938	
531	30531	Jun. 1938	
532	30532	Jun. 1938	
533	30533	Jul. 1938	
534	30534	Sep. 1938	
535	30535	Sep. 1938	
536	30536	Oct. 1938	
537	30537	Oct. 1938	
538	30538	Nov. 1938	
539	30539	Dec. 1938	
540	30540	Jan. 1939	
541	30541	Jan. 1939	
542	30542	Mar. 1939	
543	30543	Mar. 1939	
544	30544	Apr. 1939	
545	30545	Jun. 1939	
546	30546	Jun. 1939	
547	30547	Jul. 1939	
548	30548	Aug. 1939	
549	30549	Sep. 1939	

BULLEID CLASS 'MN', 4-6-2 (Built and Rebuilt)

SR	British Rail	Building Date	Name
21C-1	35001	Feb. 1941	Channel Packet
21C-2	35002	Jun. 1941	Union Castle
21C-3	35003	Sep. 1941	Royal Mail
21C-4	35004	Oct. 1941	Cunard White Star
21C-5	35005	Dec. 1941	Canadian Pacific
21C-6	35006	Dec. 1941	Peninsular and Oriental
21C-7	35007	Jun. 1942	Aberdeen Commonwealth
21C-8	35008	Jun. 1942	Orient Line
21C-9	35009	Jul. 1942	Shaw Savill
21C-10	35010	Aug. 1942	Blue Star

CLASS '8F', 2-8-0

SR	British Rail	Building Date	Name
8600	48600	Dec. 1942	
8601	48601	Jan. 1943	
8602	48602	Apr. 1943	
8603	48603	Apr. 1943	
8604	48604	Jun. 1943	
8605	48605	Jul. 1943	
8606	48606	Aug. 1943	
8607	48607	Sep. 1943	
8608	48608	Sep. 1943	
8609	48609	Oct. 1943	
8650	48650	Oct. 1943	
8651	48651	Oct. 1943	
8652	48652	Oct. 1943	
8653	48653	Oct. 1943	
8654	48654	Nov. 1943	
8655	48655	Nov. 1943	
8656	48656	Nov. 1943	
8657	48657	Nov. 1943	
8658	48658	Nov. 1943	
8659	48659	Dec. 1943	
8660	48660	Dec. 1943	
8661	48661	Jun. 1944	
8662	48662	Jun. 1944	

BULLEID CLASS 'MN', 4-6-2 (cont.)

SR	British Rail	Building Date	Name
21C-11	35011	Dec. 1944	General Steam Navigation
21C-12	35012	Dec. 1944	United States Lines
21C-13	35013	Feb. 1945	Blue Funnel
21C-14	35014	Feb. 1945	Nederland Line
21C-15	35015	Mar. 1945	Rotterdam Lloyd
21C-16	35016	Mar. 1945	Elders Fyffes
21C-17	35017	Apr. 1945	Belgian Marine
21C-18	35018	May 1945	British India Line
21C-19	35019	Jun. 1945	French Line C.G.T.
21C-20	35020	Jun. 1945	Bibby Line
	35021	Sep 1948	New Zealand Line
	35022	Oct. 1948	Holland America Line
	35023	Nov. 1948	Holland Afrika Line
	35024	Nov. 1948	East Asiatic Company
	35025	Nov. 1948	Brocklebank Line
	35026	Dec. 1948	Lamport and Holt Line
	35027	Dec. 1948	Port Line
	35028	Dec. 1948	Clan Line
	35029	Feb. 1949	Ellerman Lines
	35030	Apr. 1949	Elder-Dempster Lines

BULLEID 'WC' & 'BB' CLASS, 4-6-2 (* Rebuilt at Eastleigh)

British Rail	Building Date		Name
34095*	Oct. 1949	WC	Brentor
34097*	Nov. 1949	WC	Holsworthy
34099	Dec. 1949	WC	Lynmouth
34101*	Jan. 1950	WC	Hartland
34102	Feb. 1950	WC	Lapford
34104*	Apr. 1950	WC	Bere Alston

Locomotives Rebuilt at Eastleigh

British Rail	Building Date		Name
34005	Jun. 1957	WC	Barnstaple
34003	Sep. 1957	WC	Plymouth
34027	Sep. 1957	WC	Taw Valley
34013	Oct. 1957	WC	Okehampton
34025	Oct. 1957	WC	Whimple
34001	Nov. 1957	WC	Exeter
34017	Nov. 1957	WC	Ilfracombe
34021	Dec. 1957	WC	Dartmoor
34022	Dec. 1957	WC	Exmoor
34012	Jan. 1958	WC	Launceston
34004	Feb. 1958	WC	Yeovil
34026	Feb. 1958	WC	Yes Tor
34016	Mar. 1958	WC	Bodmin
34028	Mar. 1958	WC	Eddystone
34037	Mar. 1958	WC	Clovelly
34050	Aug. 1958	BB	Royal Observer Cc
34018	Sep. 1958	WC	Axminster
34052	Sep. 1958	BB	Lord Dowding
34045	Oct. 1958	WC	Ottery St. Mary
34031	Nov. 1958	WC	Torrington
34047	Nov. 1958	WC	Callington
34053	Nov. 1958	BB	Sir Keith Park
34029	Dec. 1958	WC	Lundy
34010	Jan. 1959	WC	Sidmouth
34039	Jan. 1959	WC	Boscastle
34042	Jan. 1959	WC	Dorchester
34046	Feb. 1959	WC	Braunton
34048	Mar. 1959	WC	Crediton
34062	Mar. 1959	BB	17 Squadron
34059	Mar. 1960	BB	Sir Archibald Sincla
34082	Apr. 1960	BB	615 Squadron
34088	Apr. 1960	BB	213 Squadron
34044	May 1960	BB	Woolacombe
34071	May 1960	BB	601 Squadron
34093	Jun. 1960	WC	Saunton
34085	Jun. 1960	BB	501 Squadron
34008	Jul. 1960	WC	Padstow
34077	Jul. 1960	BB	603 Squadron
34034	Aug. 1960	WC	Honiton
34090	Aug. 1960	BB	Sir Eustace Misser
34036	Sep. 1960	WC	Westward Ho
34032	Oct. 1960	WC	Camelford
34040	Oct. 1960	WC	Crewkerne
34100	Oct. 1960	WC	Appledore
34058	Nov. 1960	BB	Sir Frederick Pile
34060	Nov. 1960	BB	25 Squadron
34089	Nov. 1960	BB	602 Squadron
34056	Dec. 1960	BB	Croydon
34087	Dec. 1960	BB	145 Squadron
34009	Jan. 1961	WC	Lyme Regis
34024	Feb. 1961	WC	Tamar Valley
34098	Feb. 1961	WC	Templecombe
34109	Mar. 1961	BB	Sir Trafford Leigh I
34096	Mar. 1961	WC	Trevone
34108	Mar. 1961	WC	Wincanton